# ENTERTAINING AT HOME

NO NONSENSE COOKING GUIDE

# ENTERTAINING AT HOME

## IRENA CHALMERS

LONGMEADOW PRESS

ENTERTAINING AT HOME

Copyright © 1987 by Irena Chalmers

ISBN 0-681-40272-5

Printed in the United States of America

0 9 8 7 6 5 4 3 2 1

## STAFF FOR NO NONSENSE COOKING GUIDES

EDITORIAL DIRECTION: Jean Atcheson

MANAGING EDITOR: Mary Goodbody

COVER DESIGN: Karen Skelton

ART DIRECTION & DESIGN: Helene Berinsky

RECIPE DEVELOPMENT: Elizabeth Wheeler

ASSISTANT EDITORS: Mary Dauman, Dorothy Atcheson

PROJECT MANAGER: Nancy Kipper

COVER PHOTOGRAPH: Matthew Klein

TYPESETTING: ComCom, Allentown, Pennsylvania

PRODUCTION SERVICES: William S. Konecky Associates, New York

# CONTENTS

### ACKNOWLEDGMENTS

Grateful acknowledgment is made to the following for permission to reproduce or adapt original recipes:

The Almond Board; California Raisin Advisory Board; California Strawberry Advisory Board; Georgia Peanut Commission; Hellmann's and Best Foods, CPC International, Inc.; Hershey Foods Corporation; Thomas J. Lipton, Inc.; The McIlhenny Company; National Turkey Federation; Ocean Spray Cranberries, Inc.; The Quaker Oats Company and Aunt Jemima; Ms. Jane Stacey

# ENTERTAINING AT HOME

Entertaining is one of the great pleasures of life. Whether we are anticipating a cozy cup of coffee with a neighbor or an extravagant wedding for a daughter, we pin hopes and dreams on parties, reveling in the warm feeling of knowing that by welcoming our friends and families to our homes and inviting them to eat at our table, we are showing them how much we care.

It is admirable advice to relax and enjoy your own party; it is equally good advice to plan the party carefully and follow through with those plans. An organized host or hostess really will enjoy the party. A frazzled host, who remembers only at the last minute to buy ice or check on the hand towels in the bathroom, is so exhausted and nervous that the party passes in a blur.

Once you have decided on the size of the party, the time of day and where you will have it, you can work out the details. If the weather is fine you might consider an outdoor party but if you do so, make contingency plans in the event of rain. Be prepared to move inside— know exactly where you will set up the bar and the buffet table. Make sure the living room is tidy so that there will be no need for frantic picking up as raindrops beat against the window panes.

If the party is large (more than eight or ten people), send invitations that clearly ask for a response. You should know how many guests to expect; it helps in every way from shopping and cooking to deciding if it is necessary to push the couch against the wall or the dining table to the back of the room.

Make lists, lots of them. And make them days before the party. From the guest list, move right on to the menu. From the menu decide on the shopping list. Do not forget to include non-food items on the shopping list such as cocktail napkins, toothpicks, extra paper towels, garbage bags, fresh candles and transparent wrap. After you have the shopping list, make a list of chores that must be done before the party. These include everything from cleaning the bathrooms, mowing the front lawn or shoveling the porch steps, to counting dessert plates. Assign chores to different family members or special friends who are willing to help.

If the party is a formal dinner party, check on your linen days before so that, if need be, you can plan on washing it or taking it to the cleaners. If you are planning to have a large buffet, think about how the table should be positioned in the dining room. Sometimes pushing it to the wall works well, but keeping it in the center of the room facilitates more guests at one time. If you push it to the wall, raise any hanging light fixtures, to prevent guests from knocking into them.

The time of day determines the type and amount of food. An early evening cocktail party needs only finger food and dips, as guests will most likely move on to dinner somewhere else. If you ask friends in for a buffet dinner, provide plenty of food; they will arrive hungry, looking forward to a good meal.

Make as much food as possible before the day of the party. Those dishes that cannot be made in advance should be scheduled (on a list!) and readied for fast preparation. Clear out the refrigerator and freezer before you begin cooking. You will need all the storage space you can find.

Whatever you plan, keep the tone as relaxed as possible. Parties are a lot of hard work for the host and hostess but they are, above all, meant to be *fun*. If you arc calm, organized and feel in cheerful control of the party, your guests will sense this. Smiles will widen, conversations will be more forthcoming, and laughter will brighten the room. What more could a host want?

---

### THE THREE "R's" OF GIVING A BIG PARTY

RENTING

With a large enough order, most party rental outfits will deliver and pick up. Rent punch bowls, coffee urns, glasses, small tables and chairs (if you need them), tablecloths, cutlery and serving platters. Do not mix your own glasses, plates, etc. with the rental ones. Put your things away in a safe place.

RELYING ON OTHERS

Consider hiring a bartender and a waiter or two. A professional bartender will practically pay for himself just in the amount of liquor he will save you. He will know how to pour correctly proportioned drinks and will take responsibility for tapering off on alcoholic strength as the evening goes on. One bartender can easily handle 50 people.

Waiters can perform a variety of tasks, including helping prepare and pass the food, emptying ashtrays, picking up abandoned glasses and plates, keeping the bathrooms spotless, taking coats, replenishing serving trays, heating up hors d'oeuvres, and making coffee. Write out a clear, concise list of the waiters' responsibilities, including times when certain foods should be attended to, if possible.

Have the bartender and waiters come to the house at least an hour before the party begins and try to anticipate their needs before they arrive—show them where an extra corkscrew is, where you keep paper towels, brooms and dishwasher detergent, alert them to any peculiarities of your plumbing, show them where the outside light switches are and where they can find more coathangers. Tip well for a good job done.

RELAX

Spend your energies organizing the party. Once it begins, relax and enjoy your guests.

# CHAPTER 1

# A FORMAL DINNER PARTY FOR 8

Spicy Roasted Nuts

Mushroom Crêpes with Herbed Cream Sauce

Boned Roast Leg of Lamb with Herbs

Steamed Buttered Zucchini

Little Potato Pancakes

Spinach Salad with Sesame Seed Dressing

Frozen Orange Shells with Cranberry Ice

Consider using place cards for the table, so that you can be sure people with similar interests (or sparkling differences of opinion) will sit near each other. Place cards eliminate last-minute instructions about seating.

For many, a dinner party is the ultimate way to entertain. With only a few guests, the host or hostess can concentrate on a spectacular menu and take special care with the table settings and flower arrangements. To make this a memorable evening, bring out the silver, let the crystal sparkle and the fresh flowers bloom. Use your best china and most beautiful serving platters.

Make sure the candles are new and long as they probably will burn for hours while you and your guests savor each course, lingering over dessert and conversation. Have a tray ready with coffee cups, liqueur glasses and an assortment of after-dinner cordials so that you can finish the evening in the clutter-free living room.

The menu can mostly be prepared well in advance. Only the sauce for the lamb, the vegetables and the potatoes need last-minute attention. Measure, chop, slice or otherwise prepare as many of the ingredients as possible, well ahead of time. Having them at hand makes short work of the final cooking chores, allows you to feel in calm control, and gives you the opportunity to enjoy the party as much as your guests will.

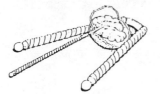

# Spicy Roasted Nuts

**Makes 4 cups**

Crisp, spicy-sweet nuts make savory cocktail nibbles.

*½ cup sugar*
*1 teaspoon cinnamon*
*½ teaspoon cumin*
*¼ teaspoon cayenne pepper*
*4 cups almonds, walnuts or pecans*
*Vegetable oil for frying*

Combine the sugar and the spices in a large bowl.

Fill a large saucepan with water and bring to the boil over high heat. Add the nuts, boil for 2 minutes and drain well in a large colander. Immediately toss the nuts with the spiced sugar until they are well coated.

You can make these up to 5 days in advance and keep them at room temperature in an airtight container.

Pour 1 inch of oil into a large skillet and heat to 350 degrees, or until a nut sizzles when dropped into the hot oil. Fry the nuts in 3 batches, for 2 to 3 minutes, stirring occasionally, until golden brown. Remove from the pan with a slotted spoon, drain on paper towels and let cool.

# Crêpes

**Makes 16 to 20 crêpes**

*2 large eggs*
*1 ⅓ cups milk*
*¼ teaspoon salt*
*2 tablespoons melted butter*
*1¾ cups unsifted all-purpose flour*
*Oil, for cooking*

Put the eggs, milk, salt, butter and flour into a blender or food processor. Blend for 30 seconds and scrape the sides of the container with a rubber spatula. Blend for 1 minute more or until the mixture is smooth. Strain the batter through a fine sieve into a bowl, cover and chill for 2 hours, or overnight.

Just before cooking the crêpes, stir the batter gently until smooth; if necessary, add a little water to give it the consistency of heavy cream.

Heat the crêpe pan over moderate heat until a few drops of water flicked onto its surface evaporate instantly. Brush the pan lightly with oil. Ladle about 2 tablespoons of batter into the pan and tip the pan until the entire surface is coated evenly. Immediately pour any excess batter back into the bowl. Cook the crêpe until it is lightly browned around the edge. Turn it with a spatula and cook for a few seconds more before sliding it onto a plate. Repeat with the remaining batter.

If the crêpes start to stick to the pan, rub its surface with a paper towel dipped in the melted butter.

# Mushroom Crêpes
# with Herbed Cream Sauce

**Serves 8**

Assemble these well before the party and heat them in the oven half an hour before you are ready to serve.

You can make crêpes a full day ahead of time, and keep them in the refrigerator. Stack with pieces of wax paper between each crêpe, and wrap the stack in foil or plastic. They also freeze well.

### MUSHROOM FILLING:

*6 tablespoons (3 ounces) butter*
*¼ cup finely chopped onion or scallion*
*1 pound mushrooms, thinly sliced*
*Lemon juice*
*3 tablespoons dry sherry (optional)*
*1 teaspoon Dijon mustard*
*1 teaspoon dried tarragon*
*Salt and pepper*
*½ cup heavy cream*

### HERBED CREAM SAUCE:

*4 tablespoons (2 ounces) butter*
*½ cup finely chopped onion*
*4 tablespoons all-purpose flour*
*2½ cups very hot milk*
*Salt and pepper*
*Ground nutmeg*
*1 bay leaf*
*1 teaspoon dried thyme*
*6 peppercorns*
*6 parsley stems*
*¼ cup heavy cream*
*1 cup grated Swiss cheese*
*16 crêpes*

To make the filling, melt the butter in a skillet over moderate heat. Add the onion and cook for 2 to 3 minutes, stirring constantly, until softened. Add the mushrooms and sprinkle with a few drops of lemon juice. Cook, stirring, until the mushrooms are softened and the moisture has evaporated. Add the sherry, if using, mustard and tarragon and cook, stirring constantly, until the mushrooms start to sizzle. Season with salt and pepper to taste.

Add the cream and cook, stirring, until it thickens and coats the mushrooms. Remove from the heat and set aside.

To make the sauce, melt the butter in a saucepan over moderate heat. Add the onion and cook until softened. Add the flour and cook, stirring, for 3 minutes. Gradually add the hot milk, stirring until the sauce is smooth. Season with salt and pepper and add the nutmeg, bay leaf, thyme, peppercorns and parsley. Cook gently for 15 to 20 minutes, stirring occasionally. Strain through a fine sieve.

Rinse out the saucepan. Pour in half the sauce and stir in the heavy cream. Return the pan to the heat and cook gently for 5 minutes, stirring constantly. Add ¼ cup of the cheese and stir until it has melted and the sauce is smooth.

Combine the remaining sauce with the mushrooms and ½ cup of the cheese; season with salt and pepper to taste.

Divide the mushroom filling evenly among the crêpes, spooning the mixture along the lower third of each one. Roll up the crêpes and put them, seam side down, in a buttered baking dish just large enough to hold them without crowding. Spoon the sauce over each crêpe and sprinkle with the remaining ¼ cup of cheese. Cover the dish with transparent wrap and chill.

About 30 minutes before you are ready to serve, heat the oven to 375 degrees. Bake the crêpes for about 20 minutes, until the sauce begins to bubble around the edges. Set the dish under the broiler for a few minutes until the cheese topping is lightly browned, and serve.

# Boned Roast Leg of Lamb with Herbs

**Serves 8**

The leg of lamb may be stuffed and rolled a day ahead.
The sauce must be made minutes before serving but if
the ingredients are measured, chopped and set out, it
is not the least bit tricky to put together.

*2 cups fresh bread crumbs*
*4 tablespoons (2 ounces) butter, melted*
*¼ cup finely chopped parsley*
*2–3 tablespoons chopped chives*
*1 tablespoon chopped fresh rosemary or*
*    1½ teaspoons dried*
*1½ teaspoons chopped fresh thyme or ½ teaspoon*
*    dried*
*2–3 cloves garlic, finely chopped*
*¼ cup pine nuts, or chopped nuts such as almonds,*
*    walnuts or pecans*
*Salt and pepper*
*1 boned leg of lamb, 4 to 5 pounds after boning*

SAUCE:
*2 tablespoons (1 ounce) butter*
*½ cup chopped onion*
*⅓ cup chopped carrot*
*⅓ cup chopped celery*
*2 tablespoons all-purpose flour*
*2 teaspoons tomato paste*
*2 cups beef broth*
*1 small bay leaf*
*1 teaspoon chopped fresh thyme or ¼ teaspoon*
*    dried*
*2 tablespoons Madeira (optional)*

*(continued on next page)*

To make fresh
bread crumbs,
grind day-old
Italian or French
bread in a food
processor or
blender.

You can prepare
the stuffed tied
roast and keep it
chilled for up to
24 hours. Remove
it from the
refrigerator
1 hour before
roasting.

To make the stuffing for the lamb, put the bread crumbs in a mixing bowl. Add the butter and toss well. Reserve ¾ cup of the mixture. Add the herbs, garlic and nuts and combine thoroughly. Season with salt and pepper to taste.

Pat the meat dry with paper towels and place it, skin side down, on a work surface. Season with salt and pepper, spread the stuffing over the meat, then roll it up and tie very tightly at 1-inch intervals with kitchen string.

Heat the oven to 350 degrees.

Put the rolled lamb on a rack set over a roasting pan, and roast, allowing 25 minutes to the pound, based on the stuffed weight. Twenty minutes before the cooking time has elapsed, remove the meat from the oven and press the remaining bread crumbs evenly onto its surface. Continue roasting for the final 20 minutes, until the crumbs are lightly browned.

Cover the lamb with a tent of foil and allow to rest for 15 minutes before carving.

To make the sauce, melt the butter in a saucepan over moderate heat. Add the chopped vegetables and cook, stirring, for 5 minutes until softened. Stir in the flour and cook for 2 minutes, then stir in the tomato paste. Add the broth gradually, stirring until thickened. Add the herbs, reduce the heat to low and cook gently for 20 minutes.

To add more flavor to the sauce, discard the fat in the roasting pan while the lamb is resting and pour the sauce into the pan. Set the pan over moderate heat and stir, scraping up the browned particles and juices in the pan. Cook gently for 5 minutes, skimming off any fat that rises to the surface. Add the Madeira and cook 2 minutes longer. Strain the sauce through a fine sieve and season with salt and pepper to taste.

# Little Potato Pancakes

**Serves 8**

A tasty alternative to the more usual potato dishes, these must be mixed and fried just before serving.

*3 large potatoes (about 1 pound)*
*3 large eggs*
*2 tablespoons finely chopped or grated onion*
*⅓ cup all-purpose flour or bread crumbs*
*1 teaspoon salt*
*Pepper*
*½ teaspoon baking powder*
*Vegetable oil, for frying*

Peel the potatoes, put them in a bowl and cover with cold water until you are ready to use them. Grate them coarsely and drain off any excess moisture.

Put the eggs in a mixing bowl and beat well. Stir in the grated potatoes and the remaining ingredients.

Heat a large heavy skillet over moderate-high heat and brush it lightly with oil. Fry spoonfuls of the potato batter for 3 to 4 minutes on each side until browned and crisp. Transfer the pancakes to a baking sheet lined with paper towels and keep them warm in a low oven while you fry the rest of the batter.

# Steamed Buttered Zucchini

**Serves 8**

Your guests will welcome this simple accompaniment to an otherwise elaborate meal. The zucchini must be steamed shortly before serving, so have the ingredients measured and ready before the guests arrive.

*2 pounds small zucchini*
*¼ cup white vermouth or chicken broth*
*2 teaspoons lemon juice*
*Salt and pepper*
*2 tablespoons (1 ounce) butter, cut into small pieces*

Rinse the zucchini and then slice them as thin as possible, using a very sharp knife or a food processor.

Pour the vermouth or broth into a saucepan. Put a vegetable steamer into the pan and add the sliced zucchini. Sprinkle with the lemon juice and season to taste with salt and pepper. Dot with butter. Cover and steam for about 10 minutes. (Do not cook too rapidly or the liquid will boil away.) Taste the zucchini and cook for another minute or so if necessary.

# Spinach Salad
# with Sesame Seed Dressing

**Serves 8**

Sesame introduces an unexpected flavor to this meal. Wash the spinach thoroughly—the minutest trace of sand will spoil the salad.

*1½ pounds fresh spinach, washed, stemmed and*
*dried*
*⅓ cup honey*
*2–3 tablespoons sesame seeds*
*1 tablespoon finely grated onion*
*½ teaspoon finely chopped garlic*
*1 teaspoon soy sauce*
*¼ teaspoon paprika*
*½ cup vegetable oil*
*1 tablespoon sesame oil (optional)*

Fresh flowers are pretty on a table but be sure the centerpiece is low enough for guests to see over it easily.

*2 tablespoons cider vinegar*
*2 tablespoons lemon juice*

Arrange the spinach leaves on individual serving plates.

Put the honey, sesame seeds, onion, garlic, soy sauce and paprika in a blender. With the motor running, add the oils, vinegar and lemon juice in a steady stream until the mixture is thoroughly mixed and thickened. Drizzle the dressing over the spinach and serve immediately.

If you are serving champagne throughout a formal meal—and more and more people are—plan on 1 bottle for each person.

# Frozen Orange Shells with Cranberry Ice

**Serves 8**

Orange shells make pretty containers for fruit sherbet or a colorful, homemade cranberry ice. If you prefer, you can use a quart of store-bought sherbet: lemon, orange or another fruit flavor.

*8 ounces fresh cranberries*
*1 cup water*
*4 large navel oranges*
*1½ teaspoons unflavored gelatin*
*½ cup sugar*
*1 large egg white*
*½ cup heavy cream*
*Orange or tangerine sections, or fresh berries*
*Cinnamon or unsweetened cocoa powder*

Combine the cranberries and water in a medium-sized saucepan and bring to the boil over high heat. Lower the heat to moderate, cover and cook gently for about 5 minutes until the cranberries "pop." Press the mixture through a sieve or a food mill and set it aside.

Cut a thin slice off the ends of the oranges so that the shells will sit upright. Cut them in half and scoop out the pulp. Squeeze the juice from the pulp and strain it through a fine sieve. Measure ½ cup juice.

Combine the gelatin, 6 tablespoons of the sugar and the orange juice in a medium-sized saucepan. Let stand 1 minute. Stir over moderate heat for about 3 minutes until the sugar and gelatin are completely dissolved.

Stir in the cranberries, pour the mixture into a shallow pan and allow to cool. Freeze for about 1 hour, stirring occasionally, until the mixture is partly frozen and mushy. Transfer the ice mixture to a large bowl and beat until smooth.

Beat the egg white until soft peaks form. Gradually add the remaining 2 tablespoons sugar and beat until stiff peaks form. Fold the egg white into the partially frozen cranberry ice.

Fill the shells with the cranberry ice, mounding it attractively. Arrange the shells on a tray and put them in the freezer until ready to serve.

Just before serving, whip the cream until it is stiff. Spoon a tablespoon of the cream on top of each ice-filled shell. Top with an orange segment and sprinkle the edge of each shell with cinnamon or cocoa.

Each place setting should include: a dinner fork, salad fork, dinner knife (blade edge toward plate) and a dessert spoon. Above the spoon and knife should be the water goblet and wine glass.

# CHAPTER 2

# AN INFORMAL AUTUMN BUFFET FOR 25

Hot Buttered Rum  •  Mulled Wine

Pecan-Stuffed Dates with Bacon

Artichoke Hearts au Gratin

Roquefort Cheese Spread

Pumpkin, Leek and Apple Soup

Corn Muffins

Alsatian Sauerkraut and Sausages

Tossed Greens with Splendid Salad Dressing

Extra-Creamy Cheesecake

A simple and satisfying menu makes full use of the bounty of autumn—the "season of mists and mellow fruitfulness." Now, when the nights are drawing in and the days are growing chilly, is the perfect time to

Several days
before the party,
clean out the
refrigerator so
that you can store
the food you make
in advance.
If you still do
not have enough
room, "borrow"
some from a
neighbor—or even
consider renting a
small refrigerator.

gather a group of good friends for a hearty buffet served before the first roaring fire of the year.

Greet your guests with a choice of warming, relaxing drinks, such as mulled wine or hot buttered     and, if you are well organized and have a large country-style kitchen, lead them directly into the kitchen where you can make last-minute preparations while joining in the fun. If your kitchen is not conducive to entertaining (regardless of the informality of the occasion), take the guests to the dining room where appetizers should be set out on the buffet table or be ready for passing. Set the table with a patterned tablecloth, colorful napkins wrapped around cutlery, and bowls or baskets over-flowing with yellow and russet gourds and squashes. Put a few pumpkins and ears of varicolored Indian corn on the table or sideboard and establish the seasonal spirit still further with a bouquet of seed pods and fast-reddening autumn leaves.

# Hot Buttered Rum

**Makes 1 serving**

Although this drink is made in individual glasses, the ingredients, multiplied according to the number of guests, may be assembled in advance. Use heavy, heat-proof glasses or mugs, and have enough long-handled teaspoons on hand so that you can put one in each glass to conduct the heat from the boiling water.

> *2 ounces dark rum*
> *1 teaspoon honey*
> *1 slice lemon*
> *3 cloves*
> *1 teaspoon butter*

*1 cinnamon stick*
*Boiling water*

Rinse a tall glass or mug with hot water and leave a spoon in the glass. Put the rum, honey, lemon slice, cloves, butter and cinnamon stick in the glass. Fill to the brim with boiling water.

# Mulled Wine

**Makes 25 servings**

Warm, spicy and aromatic, mulled wine may be prepared in large quantities ahead of time. Have punch cups or stemmed wineglasses lined up and ladle the wine into a warmed pitcher to pour. For the best results, use a fine-tasting red wine.

*3 bottles red wine*
*6 cups water*
*5 tablespoons sugar*
*¾ teaspoon Angostura bitters*
*¾ teaspoon whole allspice*
*¼ teaspoon ground nutmeg*
*1 cinnamon stick*
*8 cloves*
*3-inch strip orange peel*

Pour the wine into a large saucepan and add the water. Add the sugar and the bitters.

Wrap the remaining ingredients in a piece of cheese-c' . and tie with string. Add it to the pan and heat gently over low heat for about 10 minutes. Do not let the wine boil or all the alcohol will be lost. Discard the spices and serve the wine hot.

Don't forget to stock up on soft drinks and seltzer water. These beverages require ice and slivers of lemon or lime peel, too.

# Pecan-Stuffed Dates with Bacon

**Serves 25 (2 dates per person)**

Bacon-wrapped dates offer a piquant combination of sweet and savory and the nut in the center adds "bite." They can be prepared several days in advance and refrigerated until it comes time to cook them.

> *50 pecan halves*
> *50 pitted whole dates*
> *25 strips thinly sliced bacon*

If the pecans are large, split them in half lengthwise. Cut open each date and stuff with a pecan half. Cut the strips of bacon in half crosswise, wrap each piece around a stuffed date, and secure with a round toothpick. Put the wrapped dates on baking sheets, seam side down, about 2 inches apart. If you are not cooking them right away, cover with transparent wrap and chill.

Heat the oven to 450 degrees. Cook the dates for 10 to 15 minutes until the bacon is crisp. Drain them on paper towels and allow to cool slightly before serving.

Be sure to use wooden toothpicks if they are needed to hold food while it is being cooked; plastic melts.

---

### BUFFET TIPS

More food is eaten when guests serve themselves from a buffet table than when the dishes are served by the host or hostess. Be generous with amounts—and do not count on leftovers!

Watch the first guests at the buffet table. If their movement patterns look as though they could cause collisions, rearrange the dishes on the table.

Hours before the party, make sure you have enough serving platters, bowls and dishes for *all* the food. Never count on being able to wash the appetizer plates in time to serve the dessert!

# Artichoke Hearts au Gratin

**Serves 20 to 25**

Here is a filling, hot appetizer destined to please any guest just in from the cold. Serve it with crusty bread.

> 6 14-ounce cans artichoke hearts, drained and chopped
> 3 cups mayonnaise
> 2 cups grated parmesan cheese
> 4 tablespoons Dijon mustard
> 1 tablespoon paprika

Heat the oven to 350 degrees.

Combine all the ingredients. Spoon the mixture into 2 medium-sized shallow, buttered ovenproof dishes.

Bake for 20 to 25 minutes until brown and bubbly. If you like, you can put the dishes under the broiler for extra browning just before you serve.

# Roquefort Cheese Spread

**Makes 4 cups**

A robustly flavored cheese spread that can be made in a moment—and kept for a day or two, covered in the refrigerator. Serve it with crackers or raw vegetables.

> 18 ounces cream cheese
> 18 ounces Roquefort cheese or other blue cheese
> 2 tablespoons bourbon
> 2 teaspoons Dijon mustard

Put all the ingredients in a food processor and process until smooth. Turn out into a bowl and serve.

# Pumpkin, Leek and Apple Soup

Serves 25

If you scoop out the pumpkin flesh carefully, you can use the pumpkin shell as a soup tureen, although it is wise to fill the shell first with cold water to detect any cracks or soft spots. A 10-pound pumpkin will comfortably hold 20 cups of soup. You may prefer to make this soup with canned pumpkin, which gives a richer taste and color.

*10-pound ripe unblemished pumpkin, or 2 2-pound
    cans unsweetened pumpkin puree*
*3 pounds new potatoes, peeled and cut into 1-inch
    pieces*
*2 pounds leeks or yellow onions, sliced*
*2–3 large green cooking apples, peeled, cored and
    coarsely chopped*
*10 cups (2½ quarts) strong chicken broth*
*⅔ cup apple brandy (optional)*
*1 cup heavy cream (optional)*
*Croutons or finely sliced scallions, for garnish*

Scoop the flesh from the pumpkin and put the flesh in a large saucepan. Add the potatoes, leeks or onions, apples and chicken broth. Bring to the boil over high heat. Reduce the heat to low and cook gently for 30 to 40 minutes until the vegetables are softened.

Puree the soup in batches in a blender or food processor, or put it through a food mill.

Return the puree to the pan and reheat gently. Stir in the brandy and the cream, if desired, and cook gently for 5 minutes. Season with salt and pepper to taste and serve hot, garnished with croutons or scallions.

# Corn Muffins

**Makes 25 to 30 large muffins**

You will have to make these muffins just before serving, but if you have the muffin tins buttered or lined and the ingredients measured and ready to combine, it will take only minutes to mix the batter and fill the tins. Freshly baked corn muffins add a comforting and warm touch to this hearty meal. Serve them with sweet, creamy butter when you set the soup on the table—your guests will love them.

*4½ cups yellow cornmeal*
*1½ cups sifted all-purpose flour*
*2 tablespoons baking powder*
*1 tablespoon salt*
*¼ cup sugar (optional)*
*6 large eggs, lightly beaten*
*4½ cups milk*
*8 tablespoons (4 ounces) butter, melted*

Butter muffin tins or line them with paper muffin cups. Heat the oven to 400 degrees.

Put the cornmeal, flour, baking powder, salt and sugar in a large mixing bowl. Add the liquid ingredients and stir until just combined. Do not overmix or beat the batter vigorously or the muffins will be heavy.

Working quickly, spoon the mixture into the prepared tins and bake for 20 minutes until the muffins are firm to the touch and lightly browned.

Put crocks rather than bars of butter on the table. Crocks look attractive and keep mess to a minimum.

# Alsatian Sauerkraut and Sausages

**Serves 25**

The main course is a simple, satisfying and gloriously flavored combination of good, honest ingredients. *Choucroute garnie*—sauerkraut enlivened with spices and various other ingredients—is a traditional dish of the Alsace region of France, which is bordered by Germany and has borrowed many of its cooking techniques. If possible, use freshly made sauerkraut, bought from the butcher, but canned sauerkraut makes a perfectly acceptable substitute.

> *8 pounds fresh or canned sauerkraut*
> *1 pound thick-sliced bacon, cut into small pieces*
> *6 tablespoons (3 ounces) butter*
> *6 medium-size onions*
> *6–8 cloves garlic, finely chopped*
> *8 carrots, peeled and sliced*
> *12 parsley sprigs*
> *2 bay leaves*
> *1½ teaspoons whole peppercorns*
> *15–20 juniper berries, crushed*
> *½ cup gin*
> *3 cups dry white wine*
> *4 cups beef broth*
> *4 pounds cooked smoked pork loin, bones cracked*
> *3 pounds cooked smoked pork butt*
> *3 pounds frankfurters*
> *3 pounds French garlic sausage or kielbasa*
> *25–50 new potatoes, depending on size*

Put the sauerkraut in a colander and let it stand under cold running water for about 5 minutes to remove the excess salt. Shake the colander vigorously to make sure the sauerkraut is well rinsed, then squeeze the kraut as dry as possible, a handful at a time.

Put the sauerkraut in a heavy 12-quart casserole or a large roasting pan. Fluff it with your fingers to separate it into individual strands so that it will absorb the wine and broth.

Cook the bacon in boiling water for 5 minutes to remove the excess salt. Drain it thoroughly.

Melt the butter in a large skillet over moderate heat. Add the bacon, onions, garlic and carrots and cook for 5 minutes until softened. Stir them into the sauerkraut.

Wrap the parsley sprigs, bay leaves, peppercorns and juniper berries in a piece of cheesecloth and tie securely. Bury the bundle in the sauerkraut and stir in the gin, wine and broth. If necessary, add more wine or broth to cover the sauerkraut. Cook the sauerkraut, uncovered, over low heat for 4 hours.

One hour before serving, add the pork to the sauerkraut and turn so that the meat is completely covered. Half an hour before serving, add the sausages and turn the sauerkraut again to cover them.

Boil the potatoes until tender, peel if desired and keep them hot in a serving dish.

Just before serving, remove the herb bundle from the sauerkraut. Cut the pork and sausages into serving pieces. Serve the sauerkraut in the casserole.

Serve this with crusty bread and several kinds of mustards, such as sweet, hot, Dijon and coarse-grained.

---

## BOUQUET GARNI

A collection of herbs tied into a small bundle in a piece of cheesecloth is known as a *bouquet garni*. Traditionally, it includes fresh parsley and thyme and a bay leaf, but the ingredients may be varied and extended according to the dish being prepared.

# Tossed Greens with Splendid Salad Dressing

**Serves 25**

To estimate the amount of salad you will need for a crowd, figure on about one medium-size head of lettuce for 4 to 6 people, or about 2 loosely packed cups of greens per person. Use a variety of contrasting greens such as a mixture of romaine, watercress, arugula, escarole, red leaf and endive. Guests at a buffet will often find it convenient to put the salad on the same plate with the main course.

> *2 large eggs*
> *½ cup chopped shallots, scallions or onion*
> *2 cloves garlic*
> *½ cup tarragon vinegar or white wine vinegar*
> *2 teaspoons mild prepared mustard*
> *1½ cups vegetable oil, or equal parts vegetable and olive oil*
> *2 teaspoons dried sage*
> *½ teaspoon dried thyme*
> *½ cup heavy cream*
> *1 cup grated Swiss cheese*
> *Salt and pepper*
> *10–12 quarts loosely packed salad greens*

Put the eggs, shallots, garlic, vinegar and mustard in a blender or food processor. Turn it on and add the oil in a slow, steady stream. Add the herbs, cream and cheese, season to taste with salt and pepper, and continue processing until the cheese is thoroughly incorporated. You will have about 3½ cups of dressing.

Put the salad greens in a large bowl. Immediately before serving, toss them with just enough dressing to coat them lightly.

Store any leftover dressing in a tightly lidded jar in the refrigerator.

# Extra-Creamy Cheesecake

Serves 12

It is important to let cheesecake cool very slowly—in the switched-off oven with the door slightly ajar—so that it will not crack. If the oven door will not stay open except when fully extended, prop it open a little with the handle of a wooden spoon.

CRUST:
*1½ cups graham cracker crumbs*
*6 tablespoons butter (3 ounces), melted*
*¼ cup sugar*
*1 teaspoon cinnamon*

FILLING:
*24 ounces (3 8-ounce packages) cream cheese,*
*softened*
*½ cup sour cream*
*3 tablespoons all-purpose flour*
*1 cup sugar*
*2 large eggs*
*2 large egg yolks*
*1 tablespoon vanilla extract*
*Grated rind and juice of 2 lemons*

DECORATION:
*Strawberries*
*Red currant jelly*

Heat the oven to 350 degrees.

Put the cracker crumbs in a bowl and stir in the butter, sugar and cinnamon until well combined. Press the crumbs evenly in an 8¾- or 9-inch springform pan.

Combine the cream cheese and sour cream in a large bowl and beat with an electric mixer until smooth. Gradually beat in the flour and sugar. Mix in the eggs, egg yolks, vanilla, lemon juice and lemon rind and continue beating until smooth.

Pour the filling carefully into the crust and bake for 50 minutes without opening the oven door. Turn the heat off and allow the cheesecake to cool for at least 30 minutes with the oven door slightly ajar. Chill the cake for 4 hours or longer.

Unmold the cheesecake and decorate it with strawberries brushed with melted red currant jelly.

# CHAPTER 3

# AN AFTERNOON TEA PARTY FOR 15

Griddle Scones with Raisins

Radish Sandwiches • Chicken Salad Drums

Chocolate-Almond Tea Loaf

Walnut Tea Cake

Frosted Chocolate Jam Gems

T he revival of the afternoon tea party has come none too soon. It is a lovely way to mark the end of the day and graciously glide into evening. A late afternoon gathering is the ideal time to showcase favorite recipes for cakes, cookies, breads and tarts, as well as an opportunity to indulge in those tiny tea sandwiches we like so much, but are never quite sure when to serve.

A tradition dating from leisured Victorian days, tea used to be served to bridge the gap between a large

**33**

lunch and an even larger dinner. It fell out of favor for a good part of the twentieth century, except as a quaint custom carried on in London's smartest hotels, but today it is very much back in style. It is, in fact, the ideal meal for our times because all the food can be prepared in advance and the only last-minute need is a kettle full of boiling water. More formal than a lunch party, more relaxed than a cocktail party and more stylish than a morning coffee, teatime is an afternoon treasure.

---

### TEA TIPS

Always rinse the teapot with scalding water before brewing tea in it. This keeps the tea hotter.

Experiment with various kinds of loose tea. Allow about a teaspoon of tea for each cup—and then add a generous teaspoon for "the pot."

Never pour off all the tea in the pot; keep filling it up with fresh boiling water.

Offer guests a choice of milk or lemon slices and have a kettle of boiling water handy in case a guest asks for very weak tea.

Remember to set out a tea strainer when using loose tea.

# Griddle Scones with Raisins

**Makes about 20 scones**

Called "griddle scones" because they are cooked on a hot pan or griddle, these traditional Scottish tea biscuits are heavier and chewier than American biscuits. Serve them hot off the griddle with butter and homemade preserves.

>    *2 cups cake flour*
>    *2 teaspoons baking powder*
>    *1 teaspoon salt*
>    *2 tablespoons sugar*
>    *4 tablespoons (2 ounces) cold butter*
>    *½ cup raisins*
>    *2 large eggs, lightly beaten*
>    *¼ cup milk*

Combine the flour, baking powder, salt and sugar. Add the butter and work it in with your fingertips or a pastry blender until the mixture resembles coarse meal. (If you prefer, you can mix it in a food processor.) Add the raisins.

Stir the eggs with the milk and add to the flour mixture. If using a food processor, process with the pulse control, 1 second on, 1 second off, just until the dough forms a ball.

Roll the dough out on a lightly floured work surface to a thickness of about ½ inch and cut into 2-inch rounds, using a lightly floured biscuit or cookie cutter.

Heat a nonstick or lightly oiled cast-iron pan or a griddle over moderate heat. Bake the scones in the hot pan for 3 to 4 minutes on each side. Wrap them in a terry cloth towel as you take them from the pan. Serve them warm.

Tea sandwiches
are supposed to
be made from
small fingers or
rounds of thin
bread with all
crusts removed,
and because they
are so fragile they
should be made
no more than an
hour or two
before teatime.

# Radish Sandwiches

**Makes 24 sandwiches**

Arrange these little sandwiches on a pretty tea tray and garnish them with round red radishes with the best leaves still attached, and tiny sprigs of watercress.

> *14–16 radishes, trimmed*
> *8-ounce package cream cheese at room temperature*
> *1 tablespoon finely chopped parsley*
> *1 tablespoon finely chopped fresh chives or*
> *    2 teaspoons dried*
> *1–2 teaspoons lemon juice*
> *Salt and pepper*
> *12 thin slices bread*

Set aside the best 6 radishes to use as garnish. Grate the remaining radishes coarsely and put them in a fine sieve. Press gently with your hand or the back of a wooden spoon to remove the excess liquid.

Beat the cream cheese until it is light and fluffy. Add the drained radishes, parsley and chives. Season to taste with lemon juice, salt and pepper.

Thinly slice the 6 reserved radishes. Spread each slice of bread with the radish mixture. Top half the bread slices with an even layer of sliced bread and season lightly with salt and pepper. Set the remaining bread slices on top to close the sandwiches; cover with transparent wrap and refrigerate until firm. Trim the crusts and cut each sandwich into 4 triangles or fingers.

# Chicken Salad Drums

Makes 24 sandwiches

Curried chicken salad and crunchy nuts make these tidbits especially flavorful. To make the "drums" you will need a 1½-inch plain round cookie cutter.

*1 cup finely chopped cooked chicken*
*¼ cup finely chopped celery*
*2 tablespoons finely chopped mango chutney*
*1 tablespoon finely chopped scallion*
*1 teaspoon curry powder*
*⅔ cup mayonnaise, approximately*
*Salt*
*12 thin slices whole wheat bread*
*2–3 tablespoons milk*
*1 cup toasted sliced almonds, finely chopped*

Combine the chicken with the celery, chutney, scallion and curry powder. Add enough mayonnaise to bind the ingredients. Season to taste with salt.

Cut the bread into 48 rounds with a 1½-inch cutter. Spread 24 of the rounds with the chicken filling and top with the remaining rounds.

Combine the remaining mayonnaise with enough milk to give it the consistency of slightly thickened heavy cream, and spread on the sides of the sandwiches. Spread the chopped almonds on a shallow plate and roll the sandwiches in them, pressing gently against the plate to make the nuts adhere to the mayonnaise.

Put the sandwiches on a baking sheet, cover with transparent wrap and chill until ready to serve.

Use a serrated knife to trim the crusts from tea sandwiches. If they are slightly chilled, they are much easier to trim.

# Chocolate-Almond Tea Loaf

Makes 1 8½-inch loaf

The taste of chocolate blended with toasted almonds is a celebration in itself.

> *4 tablespoons (2 ounces) butter*
> *⅔ cup sugar*
> *2 large eggs*
> *¼ teaspoon almond extract*
> *1 ⅓ cups sifted all-purpose flour*
> *2½ teaspoons baking powder*
> *1 teaspoon salt*
> *½ teaspoon cinnamon*
> *¼ teaspoon ground nutmeg*
> *½ cup whole wheat flour*
> *½ cup milk*
> *1 ounce semisweet chocolate, grated*
> *½ cup blanched toasted almonds, finely chopped*

Heat the oven to 350 degrees. Butter and flour an 8½-by-4½-by-2⅝-inch loaf pan.

Beat the butter with the sugar, eggs and almond extract until the mixture is light and creamy.

Resift the all-purpose flour with the baking powder, salt, cinnamon and nutmeg. Stir in the whole wheat flour. Gradually add the flour mixture to the creamed butter, alternating with milk, stirring just until the mixture is smooth. Stir in the grated chocolate and the chopped almonds.

Spread the batter in the prepared pan and bake in the lower half of the oven for 50 to 55 minutes, until a toothpick inserted in the center comes out clean. Let the loaf cool in the pan for 10 minutes, then transfer to a wire rack to cool completely before cutting.

# Walnut Tea Cake

**Serves 14 to 16**

A pleasant combination of delicately flavored cake and crunchy cinnamon-spicy walnuts.

*2¼ cups all-purpose flour*
*4 teaspoons baking powder*
*½ teaspoon salt*
*1¼ cups sugar*
*8 tablespoons (4 ounces) butter, softened*
*3 large eggs*
*¾ cup milk*
*1½ teaspoons vanilla extract*
*1 cup chopped walnuts*
*4 teaspoons cinnamon*
*3 tablespoons brown sugar*
*1 teaspoon grated lemon rind*

Heat the oven to 350 degrees. Butter and flour an 8½-inch baking pan.

Sift together the flour, baking powder and salt. Beat the sugar and butter together in a mixing bowl until creamy. Beat the eggs lightly in another bowl with the milk and vanilla.

Add the milk and flour mixtures alternately to the creamed butter, gently folding all the ingredients together after each addition. The batter will be fairly stiff.

Combine the walnuts, brown sugar, cinnamon and lemon rind.

Spread half the batter in the prepared pan and cover with half the walnut mixture. Spread the remaining batter over the walnut mixture and sprinkle the remaining mixture on top. Bake for 30 minutes. Cool in the pan briefly, then cut into squares and serve warm.

Slice cakes and breads thin for tea and offer a variety of preserves, jams and butters on the tea table.

# Chocolate Jam Gems

**Makes 20 cupcakes**

These rich, dense little cakes are baked in tiny cupcake tins also known as "gem" pans. Spicy and sweet, they are delicious quite plain, or you can frost them with the Fluffy White Frosting that follows.

> 1½ cups sifted all-purpose flour
> 1 teaspoon allspice
> ¼ teaspoon cinnamon
> 1½ teaspoons baking soda
> 6 tablespoons (3 ounces) butter, softened, or solid vegetable shortening
> ½ cup sugar
> ½ cup packed brown sugar
> 2 large eggs, separated
> ¾ cup buttermilk
> ½ cup seedless raspberry preserves
> 2 ounces unsweetened chocolate, melted
> 1 cup currants or chopped golden raisins
> ½ cup chopped walnuts

Heat the oven to 350 degrees. Butter and flour 1 or 2 tiny cupcake pans so that you will be able to make 20 cupcakes.

Sift together the flour, allspice, cinnamon and baking soda.

Put the butter or shortening in a large mixing bowl and beat in the sugar with an electric mixer. Add the egg yolks and beat until light and fluffy. Stir in the buttermilk alternating with the dry ingredients, mixing just until blended.

Add the preserves and the melted chocolate and blend thoroughly. Fold in the raisins and walnuts. Beat the egg whites in another bowl until they hold stiff peaks and fold them into the batter. Spoon the mixture into the prepared pans and bake for 20 to 25 minutes or until a toothpick inserted in the center of a cake comes out clean.

Let the pans sit on wire racks for 5 to 10 minutes before turning the cupcakes out onto the racks to cool completely.

# Fluffy White Frosting

Makes about 2 cups

A deliciously rich frosting that suits tiny gem cakes or traditional layer or butter cake equally well.

> *6 tablespoons (3 ounces) butter, softened*
> *3 cups confectioners' sugar*
> *2 large egg yolks*
> *1 teaspoon vanilla extract*
> *1–2 tablespoons heavy cream*

Put the butter in a mixing bowl and beat until soft. Gradually blend in the confectioners' sugar and beat until creamy.

Beat in the egg yolks, vanilla and enough cream to make the frosting easy to spread, continuing to beat until it's light and fluffy. Add more confectioners' sugar, if necessary, to achieve the right consistency.

# CHAPTER 4

# A MEXICAN FIESTA FOR 20

Classic Margarita • Sangría

Guacamole • Chili con Queso

Nachos Supreme

Chili from the Rio Grande

Tamale Pie • Turkey Tacos

Caramel Flan

Olé! Open your doors to a group of good friends for a rollicking evening of fun and Mexican food. Pitchers of margaritas and sangría, taco chips and dips, turkey-filled tacos, red-hot chili and tamale pie all add up to a party that few people will forget.

This is happy food, full of the sunny flavors of the

great Southwest and our close neighbor, Mexico. The menu is a blending of the cuisines of the two regions— and all of it is simple, hearty and absolutely delicious. Set the table with a bright tablecloth and napkins. Bring out colorful china or buy sturdy paper plates in vibrant hues. Big, gaudy paper flowers and rough-hewn pottery will add to the charm of the evening. So, even if the weather is less than bright outside, let the sun shine on your fiesta.

# Classic Margarita

**Serves 1**

Margaritas are usually the most popular drink at a party, so you may want to make them by the pitcherful. To do so, simply multiply the quantities given here.

A jigger is one
and a half ounces.

*2 lime or lemon wedges*
*Coarse salt*
*1½ ounces tequila*
*1½ ounces Triple Sec*
*1 ounce fresh lime or lemon juice*

Chill a large cocktail glass. Spread a layer of salt on a plate. Rub the rim of the glass with 1 lemon or lime wedge and invert the glass onto the salt. Twist it in the salt so that the entire rim is coated.

Put the tequila, Triple Sec, lime or lemon juice and 3 or 4 cubes of ice in a cocktail shaker. Shake briskly and strain the mixture into the prepared glass. Decorate with a fresh wedge of lime or lemon.

# Sangría

Serves 18 to 20

A refreshing wine punch that goes well with the spicy foods of Mexico and the Southwest.

*3 cups water*
*1½ cups sugar*
*6 24-ounce bottles Rioja or other red wine*
*½ cup or more Cointreau, Grand Marnier,*
    *or other orange liqueur (optional)*
*Sliced lemons, limes, peaches, berries and*
    *other fresh fruit*

Heat the water and the sugar in a saucepan over high heat and stir until the sugar dissolves. Remove from the heat and cool. When the syrup is cold, combine it with the remaining ingredients in a tall pitcher or punch bowl filled with ice.

# Guacamole

Makes about 3 cups

Guacamole tastes best when allowed to season in the refrigerator for a few hours.

What is a Mexican fiesta without guacamole? Use ripe avocados—those that feel soft all over—and the finest tomato you can find. This, too, can be made in advance. Serve with taco chips or raw vegetables.

*2–3 ripe avocados*
*2–3 tablespoons fresh lemon or lime juice*
*1 medium-size tomato, finely chopped*
*¼ cup finely chopped onion or scallion*
*1–2 cloves garlic, very finely chopped*

1–2 tablespoons finely chopped fresh or
    canned green chilies
Salt

Peel and pit the avocados and put them in a large bowl. Sprinkle with lemon juice, both for flavor and to prevent discoloration. Mash them with a fork to the texture you like, slightly chunky or very smooth.

Stir in the remaining ingredients and season to taste with salt. Cover the surface of the dip with transparent wrap to keep it green and chill until serving time.

## Chili con Queso

**Makes 2 cups**

Here is a creamy, mildly spicy cheese dip that seems custom-made for large, crunchy tortilla or taco chips. You can make it in advance and reheat it gently just before serving.

    1 tablespoon butter or margarine
    ¼ cup finely chopped onion
    8-ounce can whole tomatoes
    4-ounce can chopped green chilies, drained
    ½ teaspoon sugar
    ¼ teaspoon salt
    2 cups (8 ounces) grated Monterey jack or
       American cheese
    ½ cup mayonnaise
    Hot pepper sauce

Melt the butter or margarine in a skillet over moderate heat. Add the onion and cook for 5 minutes until softened. Add the tomatoes, chilies, sugar and salt.

*(continued on next page)*

Cook for about 10 minutes, stirring to break up the tomatoes.

Reduce the heat to low. Add the cheese and mayonnaise and stir just until the cheese melts. Season to taste with hot pepper sauce. Transfer the mixture to a chafing dish or put it on a hot tray to keep it warm; serve with tortilla chips.

# Nachos Supreme

**Serves 20**

Since nachos disappear almost as soon as you put them on the table, it is a good idea to have several batches ready and heat only one panful at a time. This way, you can serve them fresh and hot throughout the party. Prepare them several hours ahead so that they are ready to pop in the oven.

> *60–80 large round tortilla chips*
> *4–6 cups homemade or canned refried beans, warm*
> *1–2 cups finely sliced pickled jalapeños or prepared salsa*
> *1–2 cups chopped tomatoes*
> *1 cup thinly sliced scallions (optional)*
> *2–3 cups grated Monterey jack cheese or mild cheddar*

To save room in the refrigerator, keep the loosely covered, filled pans on a cool protected porch or in the basement.

Heat the oven to 400 degrees. Have 3 or 4 jelly-roll pans or baking sheets on hand.

Spread about 1 tablespoon of the refried beans on each tortilla chip. Top with 1 or 2 strips of the sliced jalapeño or a teaspoon of salsa and sprinkle with chopped tomatoes and optional scallions.

Arrange the chips snugly on the pans. Sprinkle them liberally with the cheese and bake for about 10 minutes until the cheese melts. Serve immediately.

# Chili from the Rio Grande

**Serves 15**

Chili takes a few hours to cook, but as the time goes by, the spicy meat stew becomes more and more delicious—and fiery hot. It is a good dish to prepare the day before the party and heat shortly before serving. Remember that spices become stronger as the chili sits, so use a fairly light hand when seasoning it the first time and adjust for taste when you reheat.

Ground pure chili and chili powder should be stored in airtight containers away from sunlight. Replenish your supply often; both lose flavor after a few months.

> *½ pound beef suet, diced*
> *2 large Spanish onions, chopped*
> *4–6 cloves garlic, finely chopped*
> *4 pounds coarsely ground beef chuck*
> *½–¾ cup chili powder*
> *2 tablespoons dried oregano*
> *2 teaspoons ground cumin*
> *4 bay leaves*
> *1 tablespoon hot pepper sauce*
> *2 1-pound cans whole tomatoes*
> *½ cup tomato paste*
> *3 cups beef broth*
> *3 cups water*
> *Salt*
> *1 pound dried pinto or red kidney beans, soaked*
> *overnight in water to cover*

Cook the suet in a large heavy pot over low heat until all the fat is rendered. Discard the crisp pieces of suet.

*(continued on next page)*

Add the onions and garlic to the fat and cook slowly, partially covered, for about 15 minutes.

Increase the heat to medium-high and add the beef. Cook, stirring, for 5 minutes until lightly browned. Stir in the chili powder, oregano, cumin, bay leaves, hot pepper sauce, tomatoes, tomato paste, broth and water. Season to taste with salt.

Bring the chili to the boil, reduce the heat to low and cook gently, partially covered, for 3 hours.

While the meat cooks, drain the beans and put them in a large saucepan with about 8 cups of water. Bring to the boil over high heat, then reduce the heat to low and cook gently, partially covered, for about 45 minutes until just tender. Drain and set aside.

After the chili has cooked for 2 hours, add the beans. Cover and cook gently for another hour.

Taste the chili for salt and hot pepper sauce and add more if needed.

When you are serving food as spicy as this, be sure to have some icy cold beer, seltzer and soft drinks on hand.

# Tamale Pie

Serves 15 to 20

This mildly seasoned beef and pork mixture, sandwiched between layers of cornmeal, will please all your guests, particularly those who may prefer something a little less spicy than chili and tacos.

*1½ cups yellow cornmeal*
*1 teaspoon salt*
*1½ cups cold water*
*¼ cup vegetable oil*
*2 cups chopped pitted green olives*
*1 pound lean ground beef*
*1 pound ground pork*

*1 large onion, finely chopped*
*2 cloves garlic, finely chopped*
*Salt*
*1-pound can tomatoes, chopped*
*2 tablespoons chili powder*
*1 pound sharp cheddar cheese, cut into ½-inch
   cubes*

Heat the oven to 350 degrees. Oil 2 12-by-8-inch baking dishes.

Combine the cornmeal, salt and water in a bowl and whisk until smooth. Bring 3 cups of water to the boil in a heavy saucepan over high heat. Slowly pour in the cornmeal, stirring constantly. Reduce the heat to low and cook, stirring frequently, for about 5 minutes until thickened.

Spoon half the cornmeal into the prepared baking dishes. Keep the remaining cornmeal warm.

Heat the oil in a large heavy skillet over medium-high heat. Add 1 cup of olives, the beef, pork, onion and garlic and cook until the meat is lightly browned. Pour off the excess fat and season to taste with salt. Add the tomatoes, reduce the heat to low and cook gently for 30 to 40 minutes. Stir in the chili powder and cook for 10 minutes longer.

Spoon the meat filling over the cornmeal mush in the dishes and sprinkle with the remaining cup of olives and the cheese. Spread the remaining cornmeal over the meat filling. Bake the pies for about 45 minutes until browned and bubbling.

# Turkey Tacos

**Serves 20**

Turkey is a pleasant change from the more familiar beef tacos. Taste the meat mixture for seasoning and adjust it accordingly.

*4 tablespoons vegetable oil*
*1½ cups finely chopped onion*
*2 pounds chopped or ground fresh turkey*
*1 tablespoon chili powder*
*1 teaspoon ground cumin*
*1 teaspoon dried oregano*
*1–2 teaspoons salt*
*3–4 cloves garlic, finely chopped*
*⅛ teaspoon cayenne pepper (optional)*
*5 teaspoons cornstarch*
*½ cup water*
*1½ cup bottled taco sauce*
*20 taco shells*
*2–3 tomatoes, cut into ¼-inch dice*
*5–6 cups finely shredded lettuce*
*1½–2 cups grated cheddar cheese*

A taco shell is simply a tortilla that has been fried and folded.

If you have time and the space in the oven, warm up taco shells just before filling them.

Heat the oil in a large skillet over medium-high heat. When the oil is hot, add the onion and cook for about 5 minutes until softened. Add the turkey and seasonings and cook for 5 additional minutes, stirring to break up the meat, until it is just cooked through. Do not overcook.

Mix the cornstarch with the water and stir into the meat. Bring to the boil, stirring. When the meat mixture thickens, stir in ½ cup of taco sauce.

Spoon the mixture into the taco shells. Serve with the tomatoes, lettuce, cheddar cheese and the remaining cup of taco sauce on the side for the guests to add themselves.

# Caramel Flan

Serves 8 to 10

For best results, repeat the recipe for this rich, creamy custard, rather than doubling it to serve 20 guests.

*1¼ cups sugar*
*1 teaspoon vanilla extract*
*6 large eggs, lightly beaten*
*2 cups milk*
*1 cup heavy cream or evaporated milk*
*1 stick cinnamon*
*⅛ teaspoon salt*

Heat the oven to 325 degrees.

Heat 1 cup of sugar in a small skillet over medium-high heat. When the sugar begins to melt, reduce the heat to medium-low and cook, stirring occasionally, until the syrup turns a rich golden brown.

Immediately pour the hot caramel into a heavy, ovenproof 1½-quart baking dish. Rotate the dish quickly and evenly to coat the bottom and sides.

Combine the vanilla and eggs in a large mixing bowl.

Combine the milk, cream, the remaining ¼ cup sugar, cinnamon and salt in a saucepan and bring to the boil over medium-high heat. Cool slightly, remove the cinnamon stick, for reuse, and whisk the warm milk into the eggs. Strain the custard into the caramel-coated baking dish. Set the dish in a deep roasting pan and pour enough boiling water into the pan to come halfway up the sides of the dish.

Bake for about 1 hour, until a knife inserted in the center of the flan comes out clean. Remove from the hot water and allow the flan to cool. Cover with transparent wrap and chill for at least 3 hours.

To serve, run a sharp knife around the edge of the mold and invert the flan carefully onto a serving dish. The caramel topping will drip down the sides.

# CHAPTER 5

# A COCKTAIL PARTY FOR 50

Cocktail Punch

Cheddar Toasts • Salmon Canapés

Chicken Liver Pâté with Applesauce

Cranberry Chutney Cheese Spread

Crispy Cornmeal Crackers

Olive and Anchovy Spread • Spiced Clam Balls

T he cocktail party is still one of the best ways to keep in touch with a large number of people. While "cocktails" themselves are not specially fashionable these days, the kind of party they inspire is usually a fairly informal, relaxed, loosely structured affair that spans only two or three hours in the early evening. It is a good opportunity for the host or hostess to bring together people they think will enjoy each other, and a time for old acquaintances to renew friendships.

A party with this many guests will take its own shape. Keep the food and the decorations simple—perhaps a pretty pastel tablecloth on a buffet table, fresh flowers on side tables and in the entrance hall, and, if it is dark outside, candles in the dining room. If you want your guests to linger, consider serving a ham or turkey with baskets of rolls and breads, and a variety of mustards and flavored mayonnaise. It is also perfectly acceptable to serve only lighter fare.

When you plan a large party, send invitations that include directions to your home. Indicate whether the party will be indoors or outdoors, formal or informal.

# Cocktail Punch

**Serves about 50**

Offer a fruity, slightly alcoholic punch at a party as a pleasant addition to the expected mixed drinks and soft drinks. If you choose to make this one nonalcoholic, use lemon-lime soda rather than champagne and almond extract rather than kirsch. If you plan ahead, you can manage with only one ring mold for the decorative ice rings—make the rings one at a time well in advance of the party and keep them frozen in plastic bags until needed.

*7½ quarts (30 cups) cranberry-apple juice*
*60 whole strawberries*
*10 quarts grapefruit juice, chilled*
*2½ cups superfine sugar*
*5 quarts ginger ale, chilled*
*5 quarts lemon-lime soda or champagne, chilled*
*1¼ cups kirsch or 5 teaspoons almond extract*

Fill 5 6-cup ring molds half full with cranberry-apple juice and freeze until solid. Pour a thin film of juice on

To keep punch
manageable and
fizzy, make it in
gallon batches as
you need it, but
keep all the
ingredients chilled
and ready.

the frozen layer and arrange 12 whole, perfect straw-berries on top of each ring. Return the rings to the freezer for about 20 minutes until the strawberries are fixed in position. Add enough of the remaining juice to cover the fruit and freeze until solid.

For each gallon of punch, combine 2 quarts grape-fruit juice with ½ cup superfine sugar and stir until the sugar dissolves. Pour into a gallon-sized punch bowl and gently stir in 1 quart of ginger ale, 1 quart of soda or champagne and ¼ cup kirsch or 1 teaspoon of al-mond extract. Float 1 ice ring in the punch and serve.

# Cheddar Toasts

**Makes about 60 pieces**

An easy and tasty hot appetizer that can be assembled long before the party.

> *1 cup freshly grated sharp cheddar cheese*
> *⅓ cup mayonnaise, approximately*
> *2 tablespoons finely chopped scallions*
> *2 tablespoons finely chopped parsley*
> *2 tablespoons finely chopped chives*
> *20 thin slices of whole wheat or white bread*

Heat the broiler.

Mix the grated cheese with enough mayonnaise to make it cohesive. Stir in the scallions, parsley and chives.

Toast the bread under the broiler so that one side only is toasted. Spread the cheese mixture on the un-toasted side of each slice. Cut the bread into squares or thin fingers, using a serrated knife. Arrange on baking sheets and chill, loosely covered, until ready to cook.

Heat the oven to 500 degrees.

Bake the cheese toasts for 5 to 8 minutes until the cheese is sizzling and lightly browned.

# Salmon Canapés

**Makes about 80 canapés**

Ask the local bakery to bake you a loaf of fine-grained white bread, usually called a Pullman loaf. It is easy to slice with a long serrated knife, or, to save time, you can ask the bakery to trim the crust and slice the loaf lengthwise for you. For variety, try making canapés with other spreads such as cream cheese and chutney, highly seasoned tuna, curried egg salad or herbed goat cheese.

> *1-pound loaf unsliced fine-grained bread*
> *Lemon juice*
> *8 ounces cream cheese, at room temperature*
> *¾ pound smoked salmon*
> *Parsley, dill, sliced pimiento-stuffed olives,*
> *for garnish*

Trim the crusts from the loaf of bread. Slice the loaf lengthwise into thin slices.

Stir a few drops of lemon juice into the cream cheese.

Chop the smoked salmon into coarse pieces and then combine it with the cream cheese.

Spread the salmon-cream cheese mixture on each slice of bread and chill for at least 30 minutes until firm.

With a sharp knife, cut the slices into small rectangles. Garnish each with a small sprig of parsley or dill, or slice of olive.

If you want to serve cheese as well as hors d'oeuvres, put out no more than 3 or 4 different kinds and try to buy wheels or large chunks.

# Chicken Liver Pâté with Applesauce

**Makes 3 cups**

The combined flavors of apple, cinnamon and mace characterize this rich, smooth pâté. It is a good one to make ahead because it freezes well.

*1 cup (8 ounces) butter, softened*
*1 cup chopped onion*
*2 tablespoons chopped shallot*
*¼ cup applesauce*
*½ teaspoon cinnamon*
*¼ teaspoon mace*
*1 pound chicken livers, cut into halves*
*¼ cup apple brandy*
*¼ cup heavy cream*
*1 teaspoon lemon juice*
*1½ teaspoons salt*
*Black pepper*

Heat 3 tablespoons of the butter in a heavy skillet. Add the chopped onion and shallot and cook over medium-low heat for about 5 minutes, until the onion has softened. Add the applesauce, cinnamon and mace and cook for 3 minutes longer. Transfer the mixture to a food processor.

Heat 3 tablespoons of butter in the same skillet. Add the chicken livers and cook over medium-high heat until they are lightly browned. Remove the pan from the heat and pour in the apple brandy. Tilt the pan and ignite the brandy. Roll and tilt the pan until the flames die down and the livers are infused with the brandy.

Add the livers and the juices to the food processor. Add the cream and process until very smooth. Push the mixture through a fine strainer and let it cool.

Melt the remaining butter with the lemon juice and stir it into the cooled liver mixture. Season with salt and pepper to taste.

Spoon the pâté into earthenware crocks and cover with transparent wrap. Chill for at least 6 hours.

Push the furniture back against the wall to free up space and make moving about easier during the height of the party.

# Cranberry Chutney Cheese Spread

**Serves 20**

Easy, quick cocktail party fare that can be prepared well ahead. Because cream cheese is sold in eight-ounce blocks, it is a good idea to prepare two separate platters and top each piece of cream cheese with about a cup of the chutney. Serve with Crispy Cornmeal Crackers (page 58).

*3½ cups (28 ounces) canned or homemade*
*    cranberry-orange sauce*
*6 tablespoons golden raisins, chopped*
*2 tablespoons vinegar*
*1 teaspoon powdered ginger*
*⅛ teaspoon onion powder*
*Pinch ground cloves*
*16 ounces cream cheese*

Mix together all the ingredients except the cream cheese. Cover and chill for 4 hours or overnight.

Take the cream cheese from the refrigerator 1 hour before serving to soften. Put it on a serving platter and top with 1½ cups of the cranberry chutney. Reserve the remaining chutney for additional topping when needed.

# Crispy Cornmeal Crackers

**Makes about 8 dozen crackers**

What a good idea—make your own crackers. It takes only minutes to mix the dough and bake the crackers and the final product is so crunchy and flavorful. You will want to serve the crackers on their own as well as with dips. Bake them in advance well ahead of time and store them in airtight tins.

> 1½ cups sifted all-purpose flour
> ½ cup cornmeal
> 1½ teaspoons salt
> 1½ teaspoons dry mustard
> ½ cup vegetable shortening
> 1 tablespoon prepared horseradish
> 2 tablespoons cold water
> ½ cup sour cream

Heat the oven to 375 degrees.

Sift together the flour, cornmeal, salt and dry mustard. Cut the shortening and horseradish into the dry ingredients, using your fingertips or a pastry blender, until the mixture resembles coarse crumbs.

Combine the water and sour cream. Add this mixture to the dry ingredients and stir lightly just until the dough is dampened (the dough will be sticky).

Turn the dough out onto a lightly floured surface and knead gently a few times. Divide the dough in half. Using a lightly floured rolling pin, roll one half out so that it is paper-thin. Keep the other half covered with a damp cloth.

Cut out crackers with a lightly floured, 2-inch round cookie cutter. Put the crackers on ungreased baking sheets. Bake for 10 to 12 minutes until lightly browned, then cool on wire racks. Repeat the process with the remaining dough.

# Olive and Anchovy Spread

**Makes about 2 cups**

Try this olive and anchovy spread, reminiscent of traditional tapenade from the sunny Mediterranean. You may decide to spread it on thin toasted rounds of bread ahead of time and serve it as a canapé. Or you may prefer to spoon it into a shallow dish and serve it as a spread with a basket of crackers or some French bread.

*3 6-ounce cans (drained weight) pitted black olives*
*¾ teaspoon dried marjoram*
*12 anchovy fillets, packed in oil*
*3 tablespoons capers, drained*
*3 small cloves garlic, finely chopped*
*2–3 tablespoons oil from the anchovies*

Drain the olives thoroughly and chop them finely in a food processor with the rest of the ingredients except the anchovy oil. Remove the bowl from the processor and add the oil in a very thin stream, stirring all the while, until the mixture reaches spreading consistency. Serve at room temperature.

---

### BAR TIPS

Figure on 50 pounds of ice for 50 people. It will keep quite well in galvanized or plastic tubs as long as it is not in direct sunlight.

One fifth of liquor will pour 18 drinks. A generous host or hostess should plan on each guest averaging about 3 drinks.

Do not forget soft drinks, seltzer, fruit juice and lemons and limes; have some stirrers and straws handy, too.

Set up the bar away from the buffet table, preferably in another room. This will ease congestion and encourage the guests to mingle.

# Spiced Clam Balls

**Makes 50 balls**

An excellent idea for a party. But be warned—they are easy to eat and tend to vanish in a twinkling.

> 4 tablespoons vegetable oil
> ½ cup chopped scallions or onions
> 1 small green pepper, finely chopped
> 1 cup finely chopped celery
> 27-ounce can minced clams, drained
> 1½ cups cracker crumbs
> ½ teaspoon Worcestershire sauce
> 1 tablespoon soy sauce
> 2–3 drops hot pepper sauce

Have an urn of coffee ready toward the end of the party, even though it is a cocktail party. A cup of coffee is far better "for the road" than another sort of beverage.

Heat the broiler.

Heat 2 tablespoons of the oil in a frying pan and add the scallions, green pepper and celery. Cook for 5 minutes over medium-high heat until softened. Remove the pan from the heat and add the clams, cracker crumbs, Worcestershire, soy and hot pepper sauces.

Form the mixture into 1-inch balls and coat with the remaining oil by gently rolling them in it. Lay them on a baking sheet and broil for 5 minutes, turning on all sides until they are heated through and lightly browned. You will probably have to cook them in 2 batches; keep the first one warm while broiling the second. Serve hot.

# CHAPTER 6

# A CHILDREN'S BIRTHDAY PARTY FOR 8 TO 10

Lasagne with Meat Sauce

Monkey Bread

Tri-Color Salad • Mayonnaise Dip

Chocolate Birthday Cake

Homemade Strawberry Ice Cream

Caramel Peanuts and Popcorn

B alloons, colorful crêpe paper, noisemakers and funny paper hats are the stuff of children's birthday parties. Add to this formula rosy cheeks and big eyes bright with excitement and you have a celebration that can be rewarding and fun for both parent and child. While most young children (under age five) are content with a few presents followed by a cake with candles and ice cream, older children may want a more elaborate

**61**

Keep the party
short—1 to 2
hours is about all
young children
can tolerate.
Birthday parties
excite tots as few
other events do.
As they get a little
older, 3 hours is a
good length. Make
sure parents know
when to call for
their children.

affair. Simple games, a magic show, even a rented video are good entertainments for a school-aged child's party, but so is a well-planned meal featuring the foods that kids *really* like.

As with any party, a child's birthday party will be more enjoyable for everyone if it is carefully planned days before. Keep lists and go over them with your child. Make as much food as you can ahead of time. Figure exactly what you will need for games and be sure it is in place and ready before the party—the right number of chairs for musical chairs, a large blindfold for blindman's buff, clues clearly written out for a treasure hunt. Encourage your son or daughter to help with the decorations, tidying up the house, making the cake and setting the table.

Once the guests arrive, however, do not ask your child to do anything but have a good time—after all, it is *his* (or her) uniquely special day.

# Lasagne with Meat Sauce

**Serves 8 to 10**

Kids love lasagne and this one has a mildly seasoned meat sauce sure to appeal to their palates.

> *5 slices bacon, cut into small pieces*
> *2 onions, finely chopped*
> *4 cloves garlic, finely chopped*
> *2 carrots, finely chopped*
> *2 stalks celery, finely chopped*

2 pounds lean ground beef
3 cups tomato sauce
2 tablespoons tomato paste
1 teaspoon dried oregano
1 teaspoon salt
Pepper
12 lasagne noodles
2 cups ricotta cheese
12-ounce package mozzarella cheese
1 cup grated parmesan cheese

Put the bacon in a large saucepan or deep frying pan and cook over low heat until all the fat has been rendered. Add the onion, garlic, carrots and celery. Increase the heat to moderate and cook, stirring, until the vegetables have softened.

Add the beef and cook until lightly browned. Drain off any excess fat and add the tomato sauce, tomato paste, oregano, salt and pepper to taste. Cook gently, uncovered, over low heat until the sauce has thickened, stirring occasionally.

Heat the oven to 350 degrees.

Cook the lasagne according to the package directions for al dente. Drain the noodles and return them to the pot with a small quantity of cold water to keep them from sticking.

Spoon a thin layer of sauce on the bottom of a lightly oiled lasagne pan measuring approximately 9 by 12 by 2 inches. Arrange a layer of lasagne with the edges slightly overlapping on top of the sauce. Spread about 1½ cups of the sauce over the lasagne. Add half of the ricotta and smooth it over the sauce. Sprinkle with half the mozzarella and then generously with the parmesan cheese. Add another layer of the lasagne noodles, sauce and cheeses. Spread a thin layer of the sauce on top and sprinkle with parmesan.

Bake for 20 to 30 minutes until bubbling. Serve with the remaining sauce and parmesan cheese.

If you like, you can assemble the lasagne a day or so before the party and heat it up just before serving. If you do so, the lasagne will be cold when you put it in the oven so increase the baking time by 10 or 15 minutes.

# Monkey Bread

Serves 8 to 10

Is there a child who does not love garlic bread, the obvious and perfectly delicious accompaniment to lasagne? This is a fun way to serve it—tiny balls of bread dough are flavored with garlic butter and then baked together into a bumpy loaf. The kids can easily pull off a ball and pop it into their mouths—no knives, no messy butter. For convenience we suggest buying frozen bread dough but, of course, you can use your own homemade dough if you prefer.

> *1 pound frozen bread dough, or 2 8-ounce packages of plain dinner rolls*
> *1 clove garlic, crushed*
> *¼ cup hot melted butter*

Thaw the frozen bread dough or rolls at room temperature for 2 to 3 hours, or overnight in the refrigerator. Cut the dough into quarters and then cut each quarter into 7 or 8 pieces. Shape each piece into a ball. If you are using dinner rolls, cut each one in half and shape the halves into balls.

Drop the crushed garlic clove into the hot melted butter and let it infuse the butter for 10 to 15 minutes. Lift out the garlic and discard. Dip each ball in turn into the garlic butter.

Arrange the balls snugly in overlapping rows in a buttered 9-inch-by-5-inch loaf pan. Brush the top of the loaf with any leftover garlic butter. Set the dough in a warm place to rise for about 50 minutes until doubled in bulk.

While the bread is rising, heat the oven to 350 degrees.

Bake the bread for 25 to 30 minutes, then reduce the heat to 300 degrees and bake for 8 to 10 minutes more. Immediately invert the bread onto a serving plate.

By all means, use paper, paper and more paper when it comes to plates, tablecloths, napkins and cups.

# Tri-Color Salad

Serves 8 to 10

Most children enjoy crunching on raw vegetables such as carrots and celery. To balance the birthday meal, serve this simple salad. Depending on the age of the children and your own preference, toss the salad before you serve it with Italian dressing or serve it undressed and give them the option of dipping the vegetables in Mayonnaise Dip.

*6 cups torn mixed lettuce leaves*
*1 cucumber, peeled and cut into sticks or rounds*
*2 carrots, peeled and cut into thin sticks or rounds*
*3 stalks celery, cut into sticks or slices*
*1 pint cherry tomatoes, whole or halved*

Put the lettuce leaves in a large bowl. Arrange the other ingredients on top of the lettuce. Cover the bowl and chill until serving time.

# Mayonnaise Dip

Makes about 2 cups

*2 cups mayonnaise*
*2–3 tablespoons ketchup*
*½ teaspoon lemon juice*
*½ teaspoon Worcestershire sauce*
*Salt and pepper*

Make the dip well ahead of time and serve it in several small bowls. (Be prepared for some drips!)

Mix the mayonnaise with the ketchup, lemon juice and Worcestershire sauce. Season to taste with salt and pepper and add more ketchup if necessary. Chill.

# Chocolate Birthday Cake

Serves 12 (makes 1 9-inch 2-layer cake and about 3 cups of frosting)

Every kid on the block wants a chocolate birthday cake and this one is bound to meet with approval from the children and any adults at the party, too. The cake is splendidly chocolaty and the frosting is sweet and sugary—just the way kids like it. If your child wants "white" frosting, simply delete the chocolate from the recipe.

CAKE:

*3 ounces unsweetened chocolate*
*6 tablespoons (3 ounces) butter*
*1½ cups sugar*
*¾ cup water*
*2 large eggs, beaten*
*1½ cups sifted all-purpose flour*
*½ teaspoon salt*
*½ teaspoon baking soda*
*1 teaspoon baking powder*
*⅓ cup buttermilk or sour milk*
*1 teaspoon vanilla extract*

FROSTING:

*3 ounces unsweetened chocolate*
*12 tablespoons (6 ounces) butter, at room temperature*
*4 cups confectioners' sugar*
*6 tablespoons heavy cream*
*1 tablespoon vanilla extract*
*½ cup M & M candies (optional)*

To make sour milk, add 1/2 teaspoon vinegar to 1/3 cup of regular whole milk.

Heat the oven to 350 degrees. Butter and flour a 9-inch round cake pan that is at least 2 inches deep.

Melt the chocolate and butter in the top of a double boiler over hot, not simmering, water. Stir in the sugar and water until blended. Remove the pan from the heat and let the chocolate mixture cool. When it is completely cool, stir in the beaten eggs.

Sift the flour, salt and baking powder together. Fold the dry ingredients into the chocolate mixture. Combine the baking soda, milk and vanilla and add the mixture to the batter. Beat only long enough to make a smooth batter.

Spread the batter evenly in the prepared cake pan and bake for 30 to 35 minutes until the sides of the cake pull away from the sides of the pan and a cake tester inserted in the cake comes out clean.

Take the cake from the oven and cool it, still in the pan, on a wire rack for 10 minutes. Invert the cake onto the wire rack and let it cool completely.

When the cake is cold and ready for frosting, cut it in half horizontally with a long serrated knife.

To make the frosting, melt the chocolate in the top of a double boiler over hot, not simmering, water. Let the chocolate cool a little.

Cream the butter with an electric mixer set at high speed until light and fluffy. Reduce the speed and add the sugar, a cup at a time, making sure it is thoroughly incorporated before adding the next cup.

With the mixer running, gradually add the cream, the melted chocolate and the vanilla. When blended, increase the speed and beat the frosting until it is light and spreadable.

Put the bottom cake layer on a serving platter and spread about ½ cup of frosting over it. Position the second layer on top and chill the cake for about 15 minutes until the filling is firm.

Frost the sides and top of the cake with about 1 cup of frosting, then chill the cake until this first layer of frosting is firm. Frost the cake a second time with a more liberal amount of frosting. Press M & Ms into the frosting in a decorative pattern, if you desire. Keep the cake chilled until about 30 minutes before serving.

Circle each birthday candle with a ring of candies, or cover the cake with a cascade of colored sprinkles. Gum drops and jelly beans also make good decorations. So do jolly little plastic toys.

# Homemade Strawberry Ice Cream

**Makes 1 ½ quarts**

Have a full supply of juice or lemonade on hand. It is more refreshing than soda and better for the kids. And they like it just as well. Children play hard during parties and get thirsty often and quickly.

Freshly made fruit ice cream hits the spot when served with chocolate cake—or any time, for that matter. Be sure all the utensils and the appropriate ingredients are well chilled before you begin.

> *1 pint (about 2 cups) fresh strawberries*
> *3 cups heavy cream, chilled*
> *¾ cup sugar*
> *1 teaspoon lemon juice*
> *3–4 drops red food coloring (optional)*

Puree about 1¾ cups strawberries in a blender or food processor. Force the puree through a sieve to remove the seeds. Roughly chop the remaining strawberries and chill until ready to use.

Pour the heavy cream into the canister of an ice cream maker. Add the sugar, lemon juice and pureed strawberries.

Follow the manufacturer's instructions for making the ice cream.

When the ice cream is the consistency of whipped cream, add the roughly chopped strawberries. Stir to incorporate. Transfer the ice cream to other containers or leave it in the canister. Freeze until firm and ready to serve.

# Caramel Peanuts and Popcorn

**Makes about 16 cups**

This sweet popcorn is good snack food for a child's party. Put it out in bowls on the birthday table or when the affair is winding down. Another good use for it is to package it for the "goody" bags that go home with the young guests. If you show a video during the party, serve this as a change from buttered popcorn. It can be made a few days ahead of time.

*1½ cups roasted peanuts*
*16 cups popped popcorn*
*8 tablespooons (4 ounces) butter*
*¼ cup corn syrup*
*½ cup firmly packed brown sugar*
*½ cup sugar*
*½ teaspoon salt*
*½ teaspoon baking soda*
*½ teaspoon vanilla extract*

Heat the oven to 250 degrees.

Toss the popcorn and peanuts in a large mixing bowl.

Combine the butter, corn syrup, sugars and salt in a saucepan over medium-high heat. Bring to the boil. Reduce the heat to low and cook gently for 5 minutes. Remove from the heat and immediately stir in the baking soda and vanilla extract.

Pour the hot mixture over the popcorn and peanuts, mixing well. Spoon the mixture into 2 9-by-13-inch baking pans and spread it out. Bake for 30 minutes. Remove from the oven and cool, stirring occasionally. Store in airtight containers.

Put small prizes such as crayons, stickers, rubber balls and plastic games in goody bags rather than a lot of candy.

# CHAPTER 7

# A JULY 4 BACKYARD PICNIC FOR 10 TO 12

Yogurt Dip for Raw Vegetables

Cold Broiled Lemon Chicken

Mushroom Salad with Herbs • Carrot Tabbouleh

Cold Ratatouille

Berry Patch Shortcake

French Vanilla Ice Cream

Summer days grow pretty hot by July Fourth and they lengthen deliciously into evening. What better time to plan a small backyard picnic for the family or friends—or a combination of both? All ages enjoy outdoor celebrations, casual, carefree gatherings that encourage the generations to mingle.

Liberate yourself from the kitchen and the backyard grill for this party. Everything on the menu is served cold and most of the dishes can be made ahead of time.

Hose down the picnic table or drape a simple cloth over the porch table and set out red, white and blue paper napkins, plates and cups. Fill a pitcher with black-eyed Susans or white daisies and surround it with brightly colored platters and bowls filled with cold chicken and salads of every description. Have pitchers of iced tea and lemonade on hand, and a tub full of ice to cool off the beer.

If there is room, set up a volleyball net or a croquet course—have fun, this is a picnic!

Even if the picnic is in the backyard, think about providing a table umbrella for shade and chairs with backs for the older members of the party.

# Yogurt Dip for Raw Vegetables

**Makes 2 cups**

Vegetables are at their best in the summer and an iced bowl of crisp, freshly cut broccoli, cauliflower, zucchini, carrots, mushrooms, cherry tomatoes or nearly any other raw vegetable looks tempting set out on the porch or picnic table. Put a pottery bowl of this light, tasty yogurt dip near the vegetables.

*2 cups plain yogurt*
*4–6 tablespoons finely chopped scallions*
*4–6 tablespoons finely chopped fresh dill*
*2–3 teaspoons Dijon mustard*
*Salt and pepper*
*Sprigs of fresh dill*

Combine all the ingredients and chill until ready to use. Garnish with sprigs of dill.

# Cold Broiled Lemon Chicken

Serves 10 to 12

One of the best and easiest ways to serve chicken. Everything is made ahead and requires no last-minute attention.

> *4 3½-pound chickens, cut into serving pieces*
> *Salt and pepper*
> *1 cup (8 ounces) butter, melted*
> *Juice of 4 lemons*
> *¼ cup Dijon mustard*
> *Watercress or parsley, for garnish*
> *Lemon wedges, for garnish*

Heat the broiler.

Arrange as many pieces of chicken as will fit comfortably on an oiled broiler rack and season lightly with salt and pepper.

Put the butter, lemon juice and mustard in a bowl and whisk thoroughly to combine. Brush the chicken with the butter mixture and broil 4 inches from the broiler, basting frequently. Allow 15 minutes per side.

Let the chicken cool to room temperature. Chill until ready to serve, but take the chicken from the refrigerator 20 to 30 minutes before serving so that it can come to room temperature. Arrange the chicken on large platters and garnish with watercress or parsley and lemon wedges.

# Mushroom Salad with Herbs

**Serves 10 to 12**

Guests gravitate toward mushrooms in any guise and this salad looks especially cool and appetizing served in a bright blue ceramic bowl.

*3 pounds medium-size mushrooms, about 1 inch in diameter*
*¼ cup vegetable oil*
*1½ cups finely chopped onion*
*2 cloves garlic, finely chopped*
*2 tablespoons chopped fresh basil*
*2 teaspoons dried oregano*
*2 teaspoons dried thyme*
*½ teaspoon hot red pepper flakes*
*¼ cup lemon juice*
*½ cup dry sherry*
*½ cup finely chopped parsley*

Wipe the mushrooms clean with paper towels. Trim the stems flush with the caps.

Heat the oil over moderate heat in a stainless steel or enamel skillet large enough to hold the mushrooms in a 2-inch layer. Add the onion and cook for 5 minutes until softened. Add the mushroom caps, increase the heat to medium-high and cook for 8 to 10 minutes until softened but not browned.

Add the remaining ingredients except the parsley and increase the heat to high. Cook, stirring frequently, for about 10 minutes until the liquid is reduced to a syrupy consistency. Cool the mushrooms to room temperature. Transfer them to a serving dish, sprinkle with parsley and serve.

Picnic or not, take salads out of their plastic containers and serve them in decorative pottery or ceramic bowls

# Carrot Tabbouleh

**Serves 10 to 12**

This tangy salad is a welcome change from the more expected picnic fare. Tabbouleh can be made up to 24 hours in advance—it improves with a little "age."

Cracked wheat or bulgur is easy to find in natural food stores. Many supermarkets stock it, too.

SALAD:
*1½ cups cracked wheat (bulgur)*
*Boiling water*
*6–8 scallions, finely chopped*
*1½ cups finely chopped parsley*
*½ cup finely chopped fresh mint*
*4 carrots, peeled and grated*
*2–3 ripe tomatoes, seeded and finely chopped*
*1 cucumber, peeled, seeded and chopped*

DRESSING:
*2 teaspoons salt*
*Freshly ground black pepper*
*2 cloves garlic, finely chopped*
*1 teaspoon Dijon mustard*
*½ cup lemon juice*
*1 cup olive oil, or a combination of ½ cup olive oil
   and ½ cup vegetable oil*

GARNISH:
*Parsley sprigs*
*Lemon wedges*

Put the cracked wheat in a bowl and pour in enough boiling water to cover it completely. Set aside for about 30 minutes to allow the wheat to soften. Drain thoroughly, then spread the wheat out on a towel. Roll it in the towel and squeeze dry. Fluff up the wheat, picking up a handful at a time and letting it drift through your fingers to separate the grains.

Transfer the wheat to a bowl and add the remaining salad ingredients. Toss gently.

Combine the dressing ingredients and toss with the salad. Mound the tabbouleh in a shallow bowl and garnish with parsley sprigs and lemon wedges.

# Cold Ratatouille

**Serves 10 to 12**

With a recipe such as this, you can alter the amounts of vegetables according to what looks especially good in the market or your garden. Ratatouille is an ideal dish for a party because it improves with a little mellowing in the refrigerator. And if you are not having a party, make it anyway and eat it all week long—all by yourself!

You can also serve ratatouille hot or warm; it is an ideal dish to reheat in the microwave.

*4 tablespoons olive or vegetable oil*
*2 onions, chopped*
*6 cloves garlic, finely chopped*
*2 medium-size eggplants, chopped*
*6 ripe medium-size tomatoes, cut into wedges*
*2 medium-size zucchini, cut into ½-inch pieces*
*½ pound medium-size mushrooms, sliced*
*2 green peppers, seeded and cut into 1-inch pieces*
*2 red peppers, seeded and cut into 1-inch pieces*
*¼ cup green olives, pitted and sliced (optional)*
*¼ cup black olives, pitted and sliced (optional)*
*Handful of fresh basil leaves, shredded, or*
   *2 teaspoons dried*

Heat the oil in a large deep skillet or flameproof casserole over moderate heat. Add the onions and garlic and cook for 5 minutes until softened. Add the egg-plant, increase the heat to medium-high and stir until the eggplant is lightly browned. Add a few drops of oil if necessary.

Add the zucchini and mushrooms and simmer for about 20 minutes, stirring gently from time to time to prevent the vegetables from sticking and burning. Try not to break them up as you stir.

Add the peppers and dried basil (if you are using it) and cook for 10 minutes longer, stirring occasionally. Just before removing from the heat, stir in the optional olives and fresh basil. Cover the ratatouille and chill for at least 3 to 4 hours.

# Berry Patch Shortcake

**Serves 10 to 12**

Wash strawberries quickly and pat dry very gently, using paper towels. They absorb water easily and their flavor will be diluted if you soak them or rinse them for more than a few seconds.

You could not find a more patriotic dessert—an American original bursting with flavor.

*12 tablespoons (6 ounces) butter*
*3 cups all-purpose flour*
*½ cup sugar, approximately*
*2 tablespoons baking powder*
*½ teaspoon salt*
*⅛ teaspoon nutmeg*
*¾ cup milk*
*3 large egg yolks*
*1 egg white*
*3 pints fresh strawberries, hulled*
*1½ cups heavy cream*

Heat the oven to 450 degrees. Rub a 10-inch fluted tart pan or cake pan with 1 tablespoon of the butter.

Sift the flour, ⅓ cup of the sugar, baking powder, salt and nutmeg into a mixing bowl. Add the remaining butter and rub it into the dry ingredients with your fingertips until the mixture resembles coarse meal. Beat the milk and egg yolks together in a small bowl. Beat the egg white in a separate bowl until slightly foamy and set aside.

Make a well in the center of the flour mixture and add the milk and egg yolks. Stir just until a soft dough has formed. Working quickly, pat the dough out into the prepared pan. Brush the surface with the beaten egg white and sprinkle generously with sugar. Bake for about 15 minutes until golden. Cool on a rack.

While the shortcake is baking, slice the berries into a bowl and sweeten with sugar to taste.

Whip the cream in a chilled bowl with 2 or 3 tablespoons of sugar.

Serve the shortcake in wedges, topped with berries and cream. Accompany it with the vanilla ice cream on page 78.

---

#### MAKING ICE CREAM WITHOUT A MACHINE

If you have no ice cream maker, you can use the method known as "still freeze." Mix the ice cream, pour it into a flat metal pan and freeze until a band of the mixture hardens around the edges. Remove from the freezer and beat thoroughly with a hand beater, electric mixer, or food processor to break up the crystals. Return the ice cream to the pan and freeze again until partially frozen. Repeat the procedure 3 or 4 times until the texture is acceptably smooth.

# French Vanilla Ice Cream

**Makes 1 1/2 quarts**

A summertime party *has* to have ice cream—a good-quality store-bought one if you are short of time, or this creamy rich vanilla, homemade by you. It is particularly appropriate for a July Fourth celebration—after all, the French did help us out during the Revolution!

*4 cups light cream*
*4 large egg yolks*
*1 tablespoon flour*
*¾ cup sugar*
*¼ teaspoon salt*
*1 tablespoon vanilla extract*

Homemade ice cream increases in volume when it freezes about 30 percent, while commercial ice cream generally increases in volume by at least 50 percent.

Heat 2 cups of cream to a simmer.

Whisk together the egg yolks, flour, sugar and salt. The mixture will be slightly lumpy.

Stir the hot cream into the egg yolk mixture and return it to the saucepan. Set the pan over low heat and cook, stirring constantly, until it thickens into a light custard. Remove from the heat and add the remaining 2 cups of cream and the vanilla. Stir thoroughly and let the custard cool to room temperature.

Pour the custard into the canister of an ice cream maker and freeze according to the manufacturer's instructions. Store the ice cream in the freezer until ready to serve.

# INDEX